The

Yorkshire
Passport

Official Tyke status is hereby bestowed upon:

_____

This passport entitles the bearer on demand to pass
peacefully into the environs of the greatest county
on Earth, and to be afforded such assistance and
protection as may be necessary.

I understand that by entering God's
Own Country of Yorkshire, I am
agreeing to abide by the following motto:

The Yorkshire Motto
'Ear all, see all, say nowt;
Eyt all, sup all, pay nowt;
And if ivver tha does owt fer nowt –
Allus do it fer thissen.

Welcome to Yorkshire!

Bienvenido a Yorkshire

مرحبا بكم في يوركشاير

Welkom in Yorkshire

Witamy w Yorkshire

Mirëpritur në Yorkshire

欢迎来到约克郡

Bienvenue au Yorkshire

Willkommen in Yorkshire

ברוכים הבאים ליורקשיר

Benvenuto in Yorkshire

Fáilte go Yorkshire

یارکشائر میں خوش آمدید

Croeso i Yorkshire

Välkommen till Yorkshire

Velkommen til Yorkshire

Добре дошли в Йоркшир

...and finally: Eyup, love!

God's Own Country

The completely unofficial, 100% fake

PASSPORT

FOR NOVELTY PURPOSES ONLY (OBVIOUSLY!)

Yorkshire–English Phrasebook

English	Yorkshire
Hello	**Eyup**
How are you?	**Eyup?**
Well, will you look at that!	**Eyup!**
I enjoy your company and would like to get to know you better	**Drink up, love, tha's pulled**
I'm sure everything will turn out for the best	**Be reet**
I'm very well, thank you for asking	**Fair ter middlin'**
I'm not well at all, thank you for asking	**Nobbut middlin'**
Please move out of my view	**Tha meks a better door than a winder**

English	Yorkshire
Gosh, that is unexpected!	**Well Ah'll go ter t'foot of ahr stairs!**
Please tell me the cost of this item	**'Ow much?**
This item is somewhat overpriced	**'Ow much?!**
Please close the door	**Put wood in th'ole, was tha born in a barn?**
Golly, that hurt	**That's a threp in t'steans**
I'm terribly sorry, I don't understand	**Ah'm reight flummoxed**
I'm pleasantly surprised	**Ah'm fair capped**
Please make haste	**Frame thissen**
I have lost my wallet	**This is usually indicated non-verbally through sobs and wails, instantly understandable to any Yorkshire native**

Recipe for Yorkshire Pud

Take a Quart of Milk, four Eggs, and a little Salt, make it up into a thick Batter with flour, like a Pancake Batter. You must have a good Piece of Meat at the fire, take a Stew-pan and put some Dripping in, set it on the Fire, when it boils, pour in your Pudding, let it bake on the Fire till you think it is high enough, then turn a plate upside-down in the Dripping-pan, that the Dripping may not be blacked; set your Stew-pan on it under your Meat, and let the Dripping drop on the Pudding, and the Heat of the Fire come to it, to make it of a fine brown. When your Meat is done and set to Table, drain all the Fat from your Pudding, and set it on the Fire again to dry a little; then slide it as dry as you can into a Dish, melt some butter, and pour into a Cup, and set in the Middle of the Pudding. It is an exceeding good pudding, the Gravy of the Meat eats well with it.

The Art of Cookery made Plain and Easy by Hannah Glasse (1747)

6

The Yorkshire Anthem

Ilkla Moor Baht 'At
[sung to the tune Cranbrook]

Wheear 'ast tha bin sin' ah saw thee, ah saw thee?
On Ilkla Mooar baht 'at
Wheear 'ast tha bin sin' ah saw thee, ah saw thee?
Wheear 'ast tha bin sin' ah saw thee? [withaht thy
    trousers on]

CHORUS
On Ilkla Mooar baht 'at [wheear's that?]
On Ilkla Mooar baht 'at [wheear's that?]
On Ilkla Mooar baht 'at [wheear the ducks fly backwards]

Tha's been a cooartin' Mary Jane, Mary Jane
On Ilkla Mooar baht 'at
Tha's been a cooartin' Mary Jane, Mary Jane
Tha's been a cooartin' Mary Jane [withaht thy trousers on]

CHORUS

7

Tha's bahn' to catch thy deeath o' cowd, deeath o' cowd
On Ilkla Mooar baht 'at
Tha's bahn' to catch thy deeath o' cowd, deeath o' cowd
Tha's bahn' to catch thy deeath o' cowd [withaht thy
   trousers on]

CHORUS

Then us'll ha' to bury thee, bury thee
On Ilkla Mooar baht 'at
Then us'll ha' to bury thee, bury thee
Then us'll ha' to bury thee [withaht thy trousers on]

CHORUS

Then t'worms'll come an' eyt thee up, eyt thee up
On Ilkla Mooar baht 'at
Then t'worms'll come an' eyt thee up, eyt thee up
Then t'worms'll come an' eyt thee up [withaht thy
   trousers on]

CHORUS

Then t'ducks'll come an' eyt up t'worms, eyt up t'worms
On Ilkla Mooar baht 'at
Then t'ducks'll come an' eyt up t'worms, eyt up t'worms

Then t'ducks'll come an' eyt up t'worms [withaht thy
  trousers on]

CHORUS

Then us'll go an' eyt up t'ducks, eyt up t'ducks
On Ilkla Mooar baht 'at
Then us'll go an' eyt up t'ducks, eyt up t'ducks
Then us'll go an' eyt up t'ducks [withaht thy trousers on]

CHORUS

Then us'll all ha' etten thee, etten thee
On Ilkla Mooar baht 'at
Then us'll all ha' etten thee, etten thee
Then us'll all ha' etten thee [withaht thy trousers on]

CHORUS

That's wheear we get us ooan back, us ooan back
On Ilkla Mooar baht 'at
That's wheear we get us ooan back, us ooan back
That's wheear we get us ooan back [withaht thy trousers on]

On Ilkla Mooar baht 'at [wheear's that?] *(x2)*
On Ilkla Mooar baht 'at!

Yorkshire Miscellany

Yorkshire Graces

O Lord, who blest the loaves
    and fishes
Look down upon these twa
    wee dishes –
And tho' the tatties be
    but sma'
Lord mak them plenty for
    us a'
But if our stomachs they
    do fill
'Twill be another miracle

For God's sake go easy on
    the butter

God bless us all, an' mak
    us able
Ta eyt all t' stuff 'at's on
    this table

We thank the Lord for what
    we've getten:
Bud if mooare 'ad been
    cutten
Ther'd mooare 'a' been
    etten…

Fatther, fill mi mahth wi
    worthwhile stuff
An nudge me when Ah've
    etten enough

Yorkshire Insults

As common as muck
As daft as a brush

10

As drunk as a fuzzock
As mawngy as an owd cat
As gaumless as a goose
As thin as a lat
As bald as a blether o' lard
As fat as a mawk
As deeaf as a yat stowp

Yorkshire Sayings

Tha can allus tell a
Yorkshireman – but tha
can't tell 'im much!

I'm a Yorkshireman,
Born and bred
Strong in t'arm
And weak in t'ead!

Never ask a man if he's from
Yorkshire. If he is he'll tell
you anyway. If he's not you'll
only embarrass him.

It's a good hoss that never
stumbles, and a good wife
that never grumbles!

Yorkshire Maths

Once upon a time every dale had its own method of counting
sheep, adopted by local farmers.

	1	2	3	4	5
Airedale	era	tera	tethera	fethera	pimps
Swaledale	yan	tean	tethera	methera	mick
Nidderdale	yehn	tehn	edura	pedura	pips
Ribblehead	yah	twa	thethera	methera	pimp

Yorkshire Food & Drink

Yorkshire pudding

Voted the number one icon of Yorkshire, Sunday dinner wouldn't be the same without this world-famous batter-based culinary delight. Eaten correctly, the pudding should be large enough to fill a plate, and eaten as a starter, before the meat course.

Wensleydale cheese

Favoured by everybody from Wallace and Gromit to George Orwell, this delightfully supple yet crumbly cheese was first made in Wensleydale by French Cistercian monks. In Yorkshire we like to eat it with fruit cake.

Parkin

Outside of Yorkshire this oatmeal and treacle gingerbread cake is often associated with Bonfire Night but here we enjoy it all year round. The first published reference to parkin has been found in legal documents from West Yorkshire dating back to 1728, when Anne Whittaker was accused of stealing oatmeal to make the cake.

Yorkshire curd tart

A happy by-product of the cheese-making process, the curd tart is a case of classic Yorkshire "waste not, want not". It dates from a time when many smallholders made their own cheese and inevitably there would be some left-over curds. Sadly it is still hard to come by this tasty treat outside of Northern England.

Liquorice

Synonymous with Pontefract, the liquorice sweet was created in the 1760s by George Dunhill, who mixed the plant with sugar to create "Pomfret cakes". Liquorice allsorts were also created in Yorkshire, by Bassetts of Sheffield.

Seabrook crisps

"Lovingly made in Yorkshire" was the slogan once proudly emblazoned across everyone's favourite brand of crisps. Founded in Bradford by fish and chip shop owner Charles Brook, the name came about by accident because of an error by a clerk who wrote "Seabrook" rather than "C Brook".

Kit Kat

First produced by Rowntree's of York in 1935, this chocolate-covered wafer biscuit bar confection is one of the world's bestselling chocolate bars. More than a billion Kit Kat bars are now made in York each year.

Yorkshire Tea

First introduced in 1886 by Taylor's of Harrogate, the company remains one of the few remaining family-owned tea and coffee merchants in the UK. Celebrity fans include Russell Crowe, Patrick Stewart and Louis Tomlinson, while the tea has featured on American TV shows Friends and Homeland.

Henderson's Relish

Hendo's may not be very well-known outside its Sheffield heartland but locally it is an

iconic brand and it has been made in the city for more than 100 years.

Rhubarb

The climate of Yorkshire ensures that the world's best is grown here. The Yorkshire Rhubarb Triangle, a nine-square-mile triangle between Wakefield, Morley and Rothwell is famed for its forced rhubarb, grown by candlelight.

Ale

Yorkshire is a brewing centre for beer. Famous names include John Smith's, Black Sheep, Theakston, Samuel Smith's and Timothy Taylor.

The Yorkshire Flag

With a population of more than five million, Yorkshire has more residents than Ireland, New Zealand and Croatia. If Yorkshire was a country, it would have finished twelfth in the medals table at the 2012 Olympics. Like any country, Yorkshire has its own flag – the White Rose of York on a blue background. Its design dates from the 1960s. The White Rose of York was the symbol of the Royal House of York. It also features in the three flags for the Yorkshire Ridings, which were registered in 2013 following a competition.

Made in Yorkshire

HALIFAX

Pace®

ghd
good hair day, every day

CLOUD NINE

Provident

poundworld

MARKS &
SPENCER

first direct

How to Make a Yorkshire Cuppa

Everyone makes a brew differently, but here's how Taylors of Harrogate, the maker of Yorkshire Tea, suggest you do it, in five stages:

Run the tap a little so the water's nicely aerated, and only boil it once to keep the oxygen level up. Oxygen in water helps flavour!

Tea likes hot water, but a chilly teapot cools things down – so swirl a little boiling water around the empty pot first. For bonus points, use that water to warm the cups too.

Add two teabags to a regular teapot or one teabag to a mini teapot. If you're using loose tea, add one teaspoon per person and one for the pot. Pour the hot water in and stir a bit.

Tea needs time to unlock all its flavour, so give it four to five minutes to do its thing. This is a perfect time to munch a sneaky biscuit or daydream about holidays.

We like a splash of semi-skimmed or whole milk, but your brew is unique to you – so add milk, sugar, honey, lemon or nothing at all. Most importantly, enjoy!

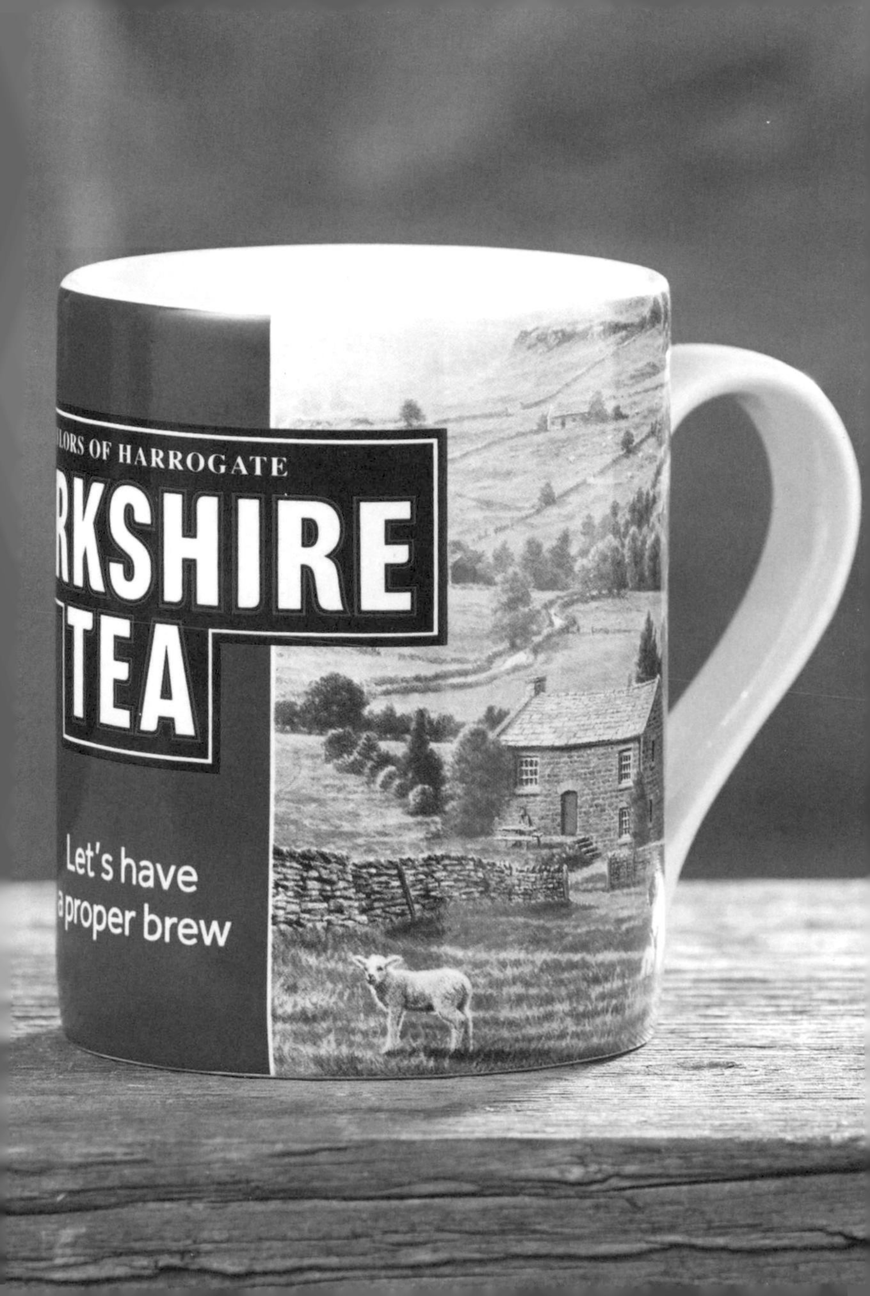
LORS OF HARROGATE
RKSHIRE
TEA
Let's have
a proper brew

YORK

Sutton Bank

MALHAM COVE

WETWANG

RHUBARB TRIANGLE

Yorkshire Dales

Yorkshire
3 Peaks

RIBBLEHEAD VIADUCT

PENNINE WAY

Crackpot

HERRIOT COUNTRY

Scarborough

Slackbottom

Great North Road

HUMBER BRIDGE

NORTH YORK MOORS

Upperthong

Bolton Abbey

HARROGATE VALLEY GARDENS

WHITBY ABBEY

LANCASHIRE
Enter at your own risk!

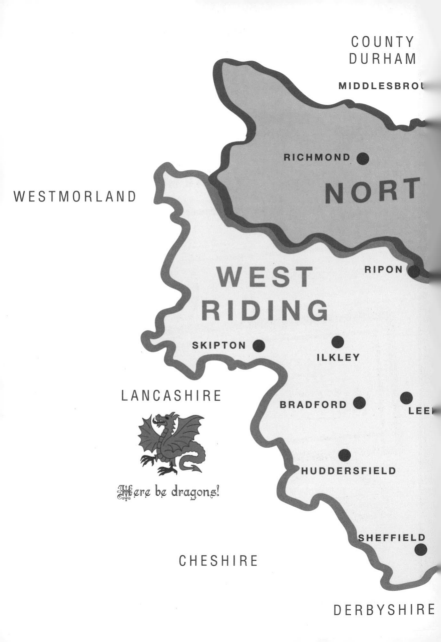

COUNTY
DURHAM

MIDDLESBRO

WESTMORLAND

RICHMOND ●

NORT

RIPON ●

WEST
RIDING

SKIPTON ●

ILKLEY ●

LANCASHIRE

BRADFORD ●

LEE

Here be dragons!

HUDDERSFIELD ●

SHEFFIELD ●

CHESHIRE

DERBYSHIRE

The historic county of
Yorkshire

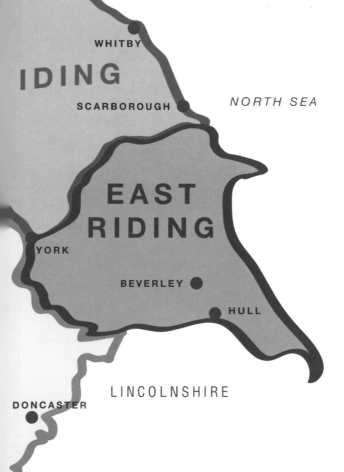

WHITBY

IDING

SCARBOROUGH

NORTH SEA

EAST
RIDING

YORK

BEVERLEY

HULL

LINCOLNSHIRE

DONCASTER

NOTTINGHAMSHIRE

Yorkshire Placenames

A pronunciation guide for speyking 'em proper

Apptrick (Appletreewick)
Barf (Barugh)
Barlick (Barnoldswick)
Bratfud (Bradford)
Brigows (Brighouse)
Bruff (Brough)
Chop Yat (Chop Gate)
Coaling (Cowling)
Gocar (Golcar)
Growmont (Grosmont)
Harwood House
  (Harewood House)
Jewsbry (Dewsbury)
Howuf (Haworth)
Keefley (Keighley)

Linfit (Linthwaite)
Massam (Masham)
Mithumroyd (Mytholmroyd)
Ollerton (Allerton)
Ootibridge (Oughtibridge)
Orkwuf (Oakworth)
Pennystun Hill
  (Penistone Hill)
Slawit or Slowit (Slaithwaite)
Slights (Sleights)
Sorby Bridge
  (Sowerby Bridge)
Suff (Sough)
Todmuddun (Todmorden)
Yorksher (Yorkshire)

Yorkshire Firsts

All these things were either invented by Tykes or made their first appearance in Yorkshire

Film-making
Club football
Rugby league
Mousetrap
Hansom cab
Catseye
Stainless steel
Manned flight by glider
Hogmanay
Surfing
Yorkshire pudding
Houdini's upside-down
   straitjacket escape
The guillotine *(the Halifax
   gibbet, pictured right)*
Ginger beer
Chip shop
Discovery of oxygen

Splitting the atom
Mapping of Australia
Abolition of the slave trade
Marine chronometer
Portland cement
Carbonated water
Hydraulic press
Beer pump

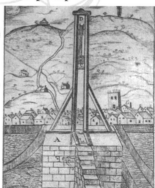

Yorkshire Films

Scenes from the following movies were all filmed in Yorkshire

Dracula (1931)

Room at the Top (1959)

Kes (1969)

Wuthering Heights (1970; 1992; 2011)

Women in Love (1969)

The Railway Children (1970)

Yanks (1979)

Chariots of Fire (1981)

A Private Function (1984)

Rita, Sue and Bob Too (1987)

The Princess Bride (1987)

Robin Hood: Prince of Thieves (1991)

The Secret Garden (1993)

Brassed Off (1996)

The Full Monty (1997)

Fairytale: A True Story (1997)

Elizabeth (1998)

Billy Elliot (2000)

Harry Potter and the Philosopher's Stone (2001)

Calendar Girls (2003)

Charlie and the Chocolate Factory (2005)

The History Boys (2006)

Brideshead Revisited (2008)

The Damned United (2009)

Four Lions (2010)

The King's Speech (2010)

The Woman in Black (2012)

Dad's Army (2016)

High-waving Heather

A poem by Emily Brontë, for all who love our beautiful Yorkshire landscapes

High waving heather, 'neath stormy blasts bending,
Midnight and moonlight and bright shining stars;
Darkness and glory rejoicingly blending,
Earth rising to heaven and heaven descending,
Man's spirit away from its drear dongeon sending,
Bursting the fetters and breaking the bars.

All down the mountain sides, wild forest lending
One mighty voice to the life-giving wind;
Rivers their banks in the jubilee rending,
Fast through the valleys a reckless course wending,
Wider and deeper their waters extending,
Leaving a desolate desert behind.

Shining and lowering and swelling and dying,
Changing for ever from midnight to noon;
Roaring like thunder, like soft music sighing,
Shadows on shadows advancing and flying,
Lightning-bright flashes the deep gloom defying,
Coming as swiftly and fading as soon.

Yorkshire Quotes

To Yorkshire cricketers it has become rather more serious than a game. It is almost a religion. (Trevor Bailey, 1961)

I want to go back to Yorkshire and the Wolds, and the smell of tarred ropes and wool, and horses in the dark barns there, and the granaries full of sliding gold and smelling of dust, the sloping field, and slow-speaking shrewd workers. (Winifred Holtby)

I find it difficult to prepare for the constant changes in the weather in the Yorkshire Dales. You awake to a brilliant morning, spend the afternoon sheltering from the tropical downpour and in the evening admire the splendour of the sunset. In New York, you can be 90% sure of the day and dress accordingly. (Allan Eady, American visitor, 1966)

I turned aside to Barnsley, famous for all manner of wickedness. (John Wesley)

Harrogate is the queerest place with the strangest people in it, leading the oddest lives of dancing, newspaper reading and dining. (Charles Dickens)

One of the charms of the Yorkshire Dales is that they are all characteristically different, like lovely sisters of the same family. (Alfred J Brown)

Saltburn is select and prettily placed; Filey quiet, Bridlington bustling; and Redcar safe... (MJB Baddeley, 1897)

The Dales air is like wine, the people generous to a fault, the going good, the views magnificent. (S Mais)

I was always very proud of living in Yorkshire, in that hilly part which is called the backbone of England, the Pennine Chain... at night I loved to see the lighted trams climbing up the dark hills like fireflies on black velvet; it seemed to me that they were brave and sturdy, like Yorkshire people, not afraid of difficult tasks or big hills. (Phyllis Bentley)

The Yorkshireman has many of the qualities of the moors on which, or on whose edges he dwells. He is often harsh, gnarled, prickly; tenacious of his rights and only roughly picturesque... (W Riley, 1920)

Yorkshire is a kingdom in miniature, with five universities, five cathedrals, mountains, moors, potholes, slag heaps, smoke and fumes and a lot of catarrh. (Bishop Eric Treacy)

The Yorkshire National Dress

Cartoon by
Tony Husband

Muffler for them
balmy (or barmy)
Yorksher summers.

Flat cap to stop
thee catching tha
death o' cowd. Must
be worn at all times
except Sundays,
even in bed.

Jacket, preferably
purchased from
Brown Muff's of
Bradford.

Pockets sewn
shut to avoid
inadvertent
access to wallet.

Yorksher kecks,
extra large for
accommodation of
one or more ferrets.
Held up wi' baler
twine – cheaper
than a belt.

Clogs – one pair
will last a lifetime.
Should always
contain a sprinkling
of Yorksher grit.

32

Yorkshire Almanac

When in Yorkshire you should find time to enjoy some of our regular festivals and customs that outsiders may find unusual. Be sure to add these dates to your diary

Driffield Penny Scramble

This revived tradition takes place on the first working day of the New Year. First recorded in the 1700s, pennies were thrown for children to pick up. These days sweets are more often thrown for local youngsters.

National Yorkshire Pudding Day

The first Sunday in February is your chance to celebrate that most famous of all Yorkshire inventions. But who needs an excuse to indulge in these tasty treats that can be eaten as a starter, main or dessert?

Scarborough Skipping Festival

On Shrove Tuesday, the South Bay foreshore is packed with people jumping up and down. It is the town's annual Skipping Day, which has been held since 1853. On this day, grown ups can skip without being thought childish.

World Coal-carrying Championships

Taking place every Easter Monday, this annual endurance test sees competitiors carry a 50kg (110lb) sack of coal for about three-quarters of a mile. The event, held in Gawthorpe, near Wakefield, has been going for more than five decades. Like the best of ideas, it was dreamt up by someone in a pub.

World Dock Pudding Championship

Held each April in Mytholmroyd Community Centre, this competition was founded in 1971 to help preserve the Calder Valley delicacy, which is made from the leaves of the polygonum *bistorta*, mixed with nettles, oatmeal, onions and seasoning, normally served with bacon and eggs.

Whitby Penny Hedge

Dating back to 1159, this custom takes place each year on the eve of Ascension Day. A short hedge made from stakes woven together, able to withstand three tides, is constructed on the shore at Whitby, near the harbour.

Great Knaresborough Bed Race

First staged in 1966, this popular event held on the second Saturday in June combines a fancy dress pageant with a gruelling time trial, ending with a swim through the icy River Nidd. Ninety teams of six runners and a passenger compete each year, with the competitiors all vying for the coveted "Best Dressed Team" award.

Oxenhope Straw Race
The race, which takes place every July, was started in 1976 by two men who made a bet about racing from one pub to another carrying a bale of straw. The tradition has carried on ever since, raising hundreds of thousands of pounds for charity. These days the straw is carried by teams of two.

Yorkshire Day
Every August 1, the county is bedecked with Yorkshire flags as residents celebrate living in the world's greatest county. Founded in the 1970s by the Yorkshire Ridings Society, to promote the historic county boundaries, the day has grown in popularity recently.

Kettlewell Scarecrow Festival
Every August the Wharfedale village of Kettlewell is filled with scarecrows, all dressed to that year's theme. Founded in 1994, the festival has grown into a huge visitor attraction.

Egton Bridge Gooseberry Show
Held on the first Tuesday in August by the Egton Bridge Old Gooseberry Society, Britain's oldest surviving

gooseberry show was founded in 1800. In 2009, a berry weighed in at 2.19 oz, making it the heaviest ever shown in the UK. It has since been recognised as an official world record.

Burning of Bartle

On the Saturday nearest St Bartholomew's Day (August 24) a larger-than-life effigy of "Bartle" is paraded around the village of West Witton in Wensleydale, complete with glowing eyes. It ends up at Grasgill End, where the effigy is burnt.

Richmond Ceremony of the First Fruits

The ancient custom of the First Fruits is held in Richmond each harvest. A local farmer presents to the mayor a small sackful of newly threshed corn. This the mayor hands to a miller, who examines the corn, and passes judgement on its quality.

Sowerby Bridge Rushbearing

The first modern Rushbearing was held in 1977, reviving an ancient tradition. Taking place during the first weekend in September, the focal point of the event is the sixteen-foot high two-wheeled decorated and thatched "rushcart", which is pulled by sixty local men dressed in Panama hats, white shirts, black trousers and clogs.

Scroggling the Holly

Marking the start of the festive season in Haworth, this ceremony takes place in late November or early December. It involves gathering holly to decorate the village. Locals in Victorian dress lead a parade.

Richmond Christmas Shilling

Every December, specially minted coins are distributed to pensioners at a ceremony in Richmond Town Hall. The custom dates back to the sixteenth century when provision was made for donations to the town's elderly and poor.

Handsworth Sword Dance

Every Boxing Day, in Sheffield, the Handsworth Traditional Sword Dancers perform their intricate dance, featuring a "lock" of intertwined swords.

Yorkshire's Best Views

The top ten views in Yorkshire, as voted for by readers of *Dalesman* magazine

More than 1,100 votes were cast.

1. From Sutton Bank/ Whitestonecliffe

The choice of this view as Yorkshire's best is hardly controversial. Indeed, many would argue it is not only the best in Yorkshire, but the best in Britain too. James Herriot loved the view so much his ashes were scattered here. Of what he insisted was the "finest view in England" he wrote, "No place better for a short stroll – along the green path which winds round the hill's edge with the fresh wind swirling and that incredible panorama beneath."

2. Ribblehead Viaduct

Ribblehead Viaduct is a popular subject for many artists, including Masham-based Ian Scott Massie. "When I first came to the Dales I was blown away by the beauty of the landscape," he said. "Swaledale and then Wensleydale opened up before me: tiny barns in the corners of green and buttercup fields, clusters of ash trees overhanging rambling stone farmhouses and the ever-present drystone walls. But as we drove from Hawes, through Widdale, something amazing appeared – the Ribblehead Viaduct."

3. Whitby Harbour from the 199 Steps

To enjoy the best views you have to work up a bit of a sweat and this is certainly the case with the view that took third place in our poll. Every year, thousands of visitors from all over the world clamber up Whitby's famous 199 Steps.

They put themselves through this exertion primarily for two reasons – to count the steps and to enjoy the spectacular view from the top.

4. Robin Hood's Bay from Ravenscar

With views like this, is it any wonder the Victorians dreamed of turning Ravenscar into a seaside resort to rival Scarborough? Robin Hood's Bay, once a haunt of smugglers, is one of the most picturesque villages in the country.

5. Muker hay meadows

To modern eyes the astounding range of colours and textures of Muker's hay

Sutton Bank, Yorkshire's favourite view

meadows are stunningly beautiful, but visitors to Swaledale in bygone times weren't always so impressed. In the influential A Month in Yorkshire (1858), Walter White seems underwhelmed: "Still nothing but grass in the fields; and the same all the way to Reeth," is all he had to say about the Muker countryside.

6. Buttertubs Pass

Drivers in the Dales will immediately recognise this view, but it is now perhaps best known for providing a spectacular backdrop to the 2014 Tour de France.

7. Whitby Abbey

The atmospheric ruins of this Benedictine abbey overlooking the sea are said to have inspired Bram Stoker while writing *Dracula*.

8. Burnsall

This unspoilt Wharfedale village, with its five-arch bridge, is picture-perfect all year round.

9. Swaledale from Crackpot Hall

A spectacular view down the dale can be had from this ruined farmhouse.

10. Bolton Abbey

The idyllic location of this ruined abbey has made it very popular with artists. The view has been painted by Turner and Landseer and it inspired a Wordsworth poem.

The Dales' Five Senses

An unattributed poem from 1944

Seeing:
Cloud shadows chasing upon hill country.
The blue shadows of sunlit snow.
A full moon bathing the roofs of a sleeping village.

Hearing:
The running waters on rocky streams.
The distant noise of railway trains, now puffing and
clanking up, now rattling down, a long incline.
The piping and crying of curlews.

Smelling:
Heather in full bloom on a dry, warm day.
In the fields: broad beans in flower; new-mown hay.

Tasting:
A farmhouse tea of home-cured ham and eggs.
Well-matured Yorkshire parkin.

Feeling:
A west wind when walking on the high hills.
The glow of the face, neck and hands after a long day
out in the sun and the wind.

Most of this costs little or nowt, and so does exploring Nature.

In t'Beginning

In't beginning there was nowt and God said, "Let theer be leet" and there was leet and He could see fer miles.

On't fust day, God created Yorkshire, and he looked and He sayeth, "It is good."

On't second day, He created t'beeasts of t'field and t'air – whippets, lurchers and pigeons – and He sayeth, "It is good."

On't third day he created Yorkshireman, who was strong in t'arm and could call a spade a shovel, ter hold dominion over Yorkshire and beeasts of t'field and t'fowls in t'air and ter look out fer Yorkshire, and He sayeth, "It is good."

On't fourth day, He created Yorkshirelass, who were fair of face, and strong in t'arm, who could make Yorkshire puds, and skivvy for t'Yorkshireman. And He looked and sayeth, "It is good."

On't fifth day, He created t'oceans, the fairest of them being t'North Sea, thet filled the coastline of Yorkshire with unlimited beauty and provided fish fer t'Yorkshireman and his Lass. And He looked and He sayeth, "It is good."

On t'Sixth day, He created t'rest of t'world and as He was running out of ideas, He created Lancashire.

And He looked, and He

looked again, and He sayeth, "By heck, after all this work, I think I need a day off."

Mike O'Dowd, *Dalesman,* **May 2014**

T'Lord's Prayer

Ahr Fatther, 'oo art in 'Eaven, let thy name bi shown respect,
Let thy Kingdom come abaht –
An' what tha wants doin', Lord, let it be done –
'Ere on Earth, same as up yonder;
Gi'e us each day summat to eyt an' sup
An' let us off, Lord,
If we've offended Thee bi doin' owt wrong –
An' 'elp us nut to 'od grudges agen other fowk
If they've done owt to offend us;
An' keep us aht o' t' rooad o' temptation,
An' aht o' t' clutches of Owd Nick,
Fer it's all thine is t' Kingdom, Lord,
An' all t' Pahr, an' all t' Glooary,
Fer ivver an' ivver...
Aye! It is that!

Adapted by Arnold Kellett

Citizenship Test

1. What do you call a bread roll?
☐ a) Bread cake
☐ b) Teacake
☐ c) Scuffler
☐ d) Any of the above

2. Which of these is not one of the Ridings?
☐ a) North Riding
☐ b) East Riding
☐ c) South Riding
☐ d) West Riding

3. Where would you find a ginnel?
☐ a) On the beach
☐ b) In your shed
☐ c) Bottom of a pint glass
☐ d) Between two houses

4. "Baht 'at" means...?
☐ a) To belch loudly

☐ b) Without a hat
☐ c) About town
☐ d) Brown bread

5. What must always be eaten with Christmas cake?
☐ a) Icing
☐ b) Gravy
☐ c) Custard
☐ d) Cheese

6. When is dinner?
☐ a) Before tea
☐ b) After tea
☐ c) After lunch
☐ d) Only on a Sunday

7. What are kecks?
☐ a) Cream cakes
☐ b) Trousers
☐ c) Kestrels
☐ d) Shoes

8. What is a Fat Rascal?
☐ a) A rotund robber
☐ b) A spare tyre
☐ c) Brian Blessed
☐ d) A tasty delicacy

9. Who won the War of the Roses?
☐ a) Yorkshire
☐ b) Lancashire
☐ c) Rose McGowan
☐ d) It never ended

10. What is the answer to all life's problems?
☐ a) God
☐ b) Death
☐ c) Mindfulness
☐ d) A nice cup of tea

11. If someone is mardy, they are...?
☐ a) Overweight
☐ b) Fun
☐ c) Miserable
☐ d) A big fan of Tuesdays

12. When do you put the central heating on?
☐ a) November
☐ b) December
☐ c) Not till it snows
☐ d) Central what?

Answers: 1. d), 2. c), 3. d), 4. b), 5. d), 6. a), 7. b), 8. d), 9. d), 10. d), 11. c), 12. d)

Image credits

Yorkshire rose (cover and watermark): CC BY-SA 3.0; House of York Coat of Arms (p2): CC BY-SA 3.0; Yorkshire pudding (p6) © Ewan Munro: CC BY-SA 2.0; Yorkshire flag (p15): public domain; Yorkshire Tea mug (p19) © Yorkshire Tea; Halifax gibbet (p27): public domain; Yorkshire costume (p32) © Tony Husband; Wheat (p36): public domain; Sutton Bank (pp40–41) © Welcome to Yorkshire. All logos on pages 16–17 belong to the copyright holders All other images © Country Publications Ltd

Publisher information

First published in 2016 by Dalesman, an imprint of Country Publications Ltd
The Water Mill, Broughton Hall, Skipton, North Yorkshire BD23 3AG
www.dalesman.co.uk

Reprinted 2017 (twice), 2018

Design and text © Adrian Braddy and Lisa Firth 2016
Additional material © Copyright holders as stated 2016

ISBN 978-1-85568-357-0

Typeset in Goudy Old Style.
Printed in China for Latitude Press.